Wonderful Woodlice and Other Incredible Isopods

David R Morgan

illustrated by Oksana Reha

A2Z PRESS

Wonderful Woodlice and Other Incredible Isopods

Printed in the United States of America

A 2 Z Press LLC

PO Box 582

Deleon Springs, FL 32130

bestlittleonlinebookstore.com

sizemore3630@aol.com

440-241-3126

ISBN: 978-1-954191-67-9

Dedication

To Bex and Toby
Who are incredibly
wonderful in so
many varied ways!
and to Sue,
for her continuing
friendship

This book belongs to:

_____

Isopods have been around for at least 300 million years,

Some can roll themselves into a ball,
to combat all their fears.

They are the only crustaceans
where many live on land,
They nicely help Mother Nature break down
things in her forests, plains, and sand.

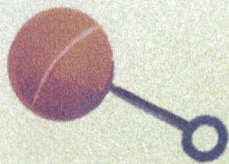

Babies come into the world looking
just like their parent isopod.
Yes, exactly the same, no matter how odd.

Now, creatures like tiny woodlice
are the isopods' cousins.
In Spring and Summer, they
lay eggs by the dozens.

Woodlice go by so many nick-names:
Like chuggy pigs, doodlebugs,
pill bugs, rolly goes,
and cheesy bug, boat-builder,
stinky-pigs, even tiny tumbling-armadillos!

Crustaceans
Isopoda

rollygoes

OTHER NAMES FOR WOODLICE

stinky-pigs

LAND

cheesy bug

boat-builder

tumbling armadillos

WATER

Crustaceans - including woodlice - form the
Order, 'Isopoda,' you can plainly see,
And isopods can be found anywhere - on land,
in freshwater, or in the salty sea.

Woodlice have fourteen jointed limbs,
with an 'exoskeleton'
(outside skeleton) like crabs.

1, 2,... 14!

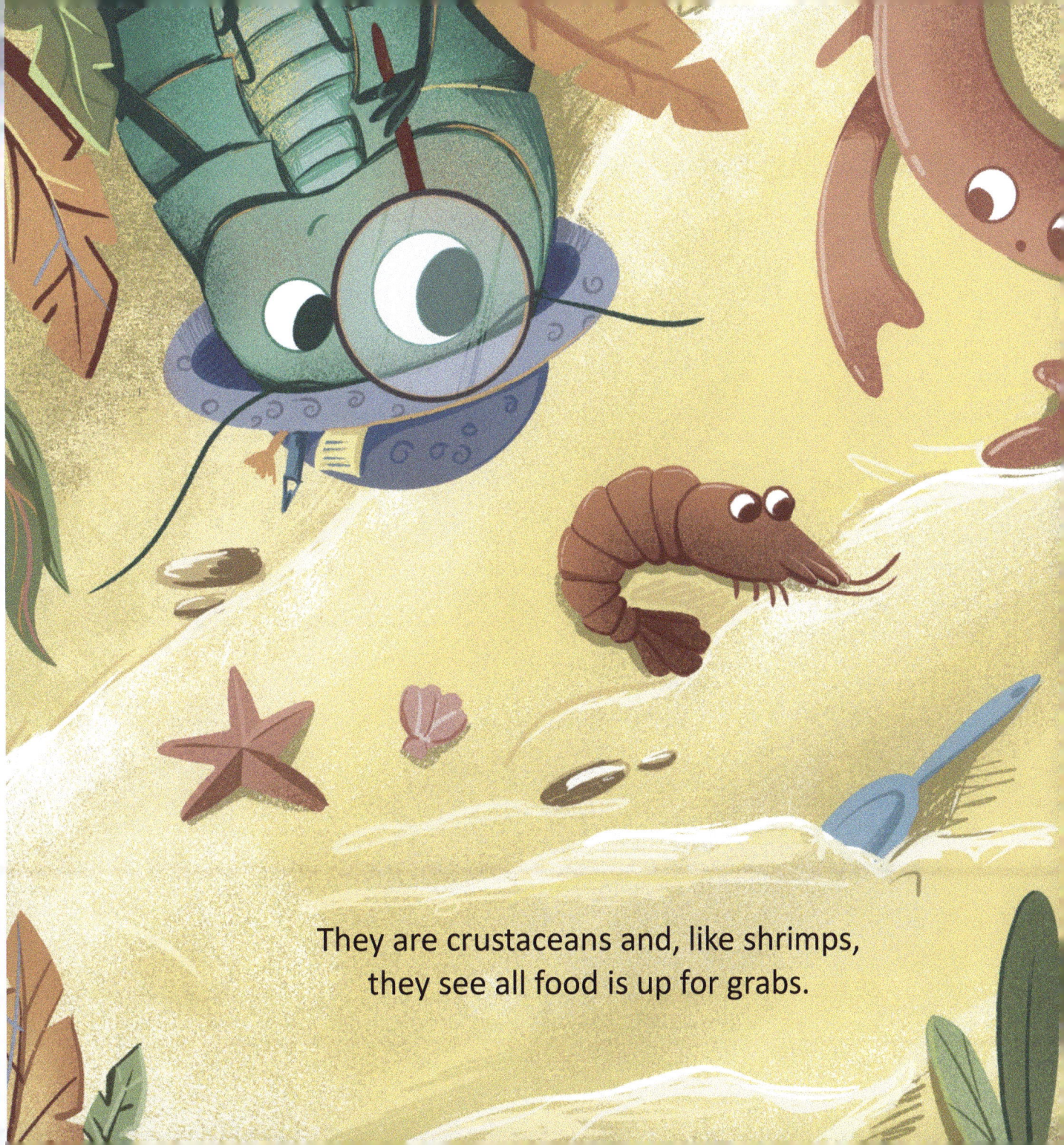

They are crustaceans and, like shrimps,
they see all food is up for grabs.

Breathing with "lungs"
on their hind legs is a
very neat trick.

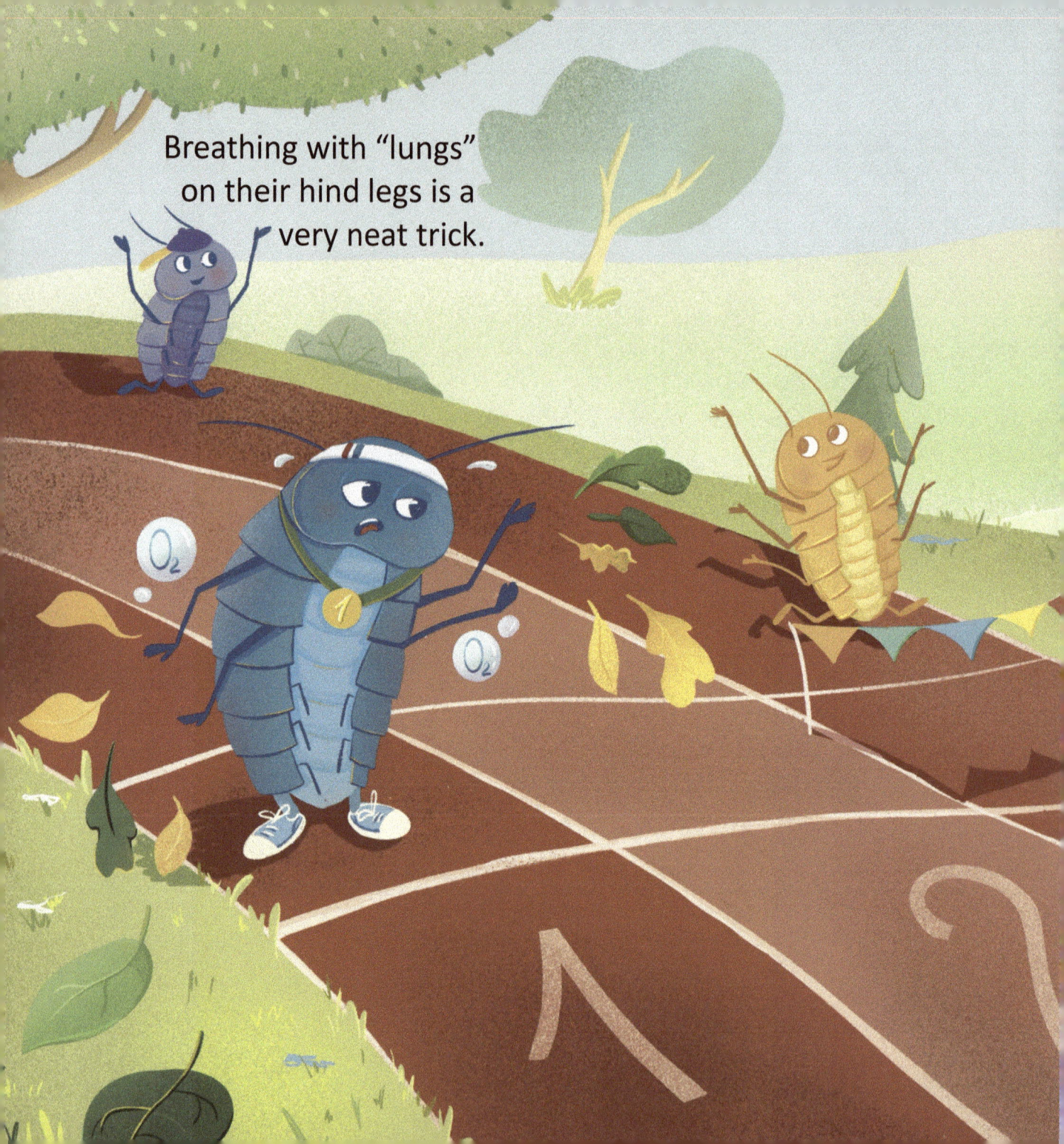

And woodlice are only 0.1-1.1 inches in size, but these guys can move really quick!

"Mum, each woodlouse looks like
a muddy Medieval knight,
They stay well-hidden when they keep
their armour dull, not bright!"

"Yes, dear. And, when threatened, they
will suddenly curl up like a pill,
Safe and sound in their armour,
keeping silent and still."

Harmless to humans are these
'invertebrates' - creatures
without a backbone.
They can find shelter under a fallen
autumn leaf or any small stone!

They can live for four years in your garden
and may even visit your house.
And just so you know, a *group* are called
'woodlice' and *one* is a 'woodlouse.'

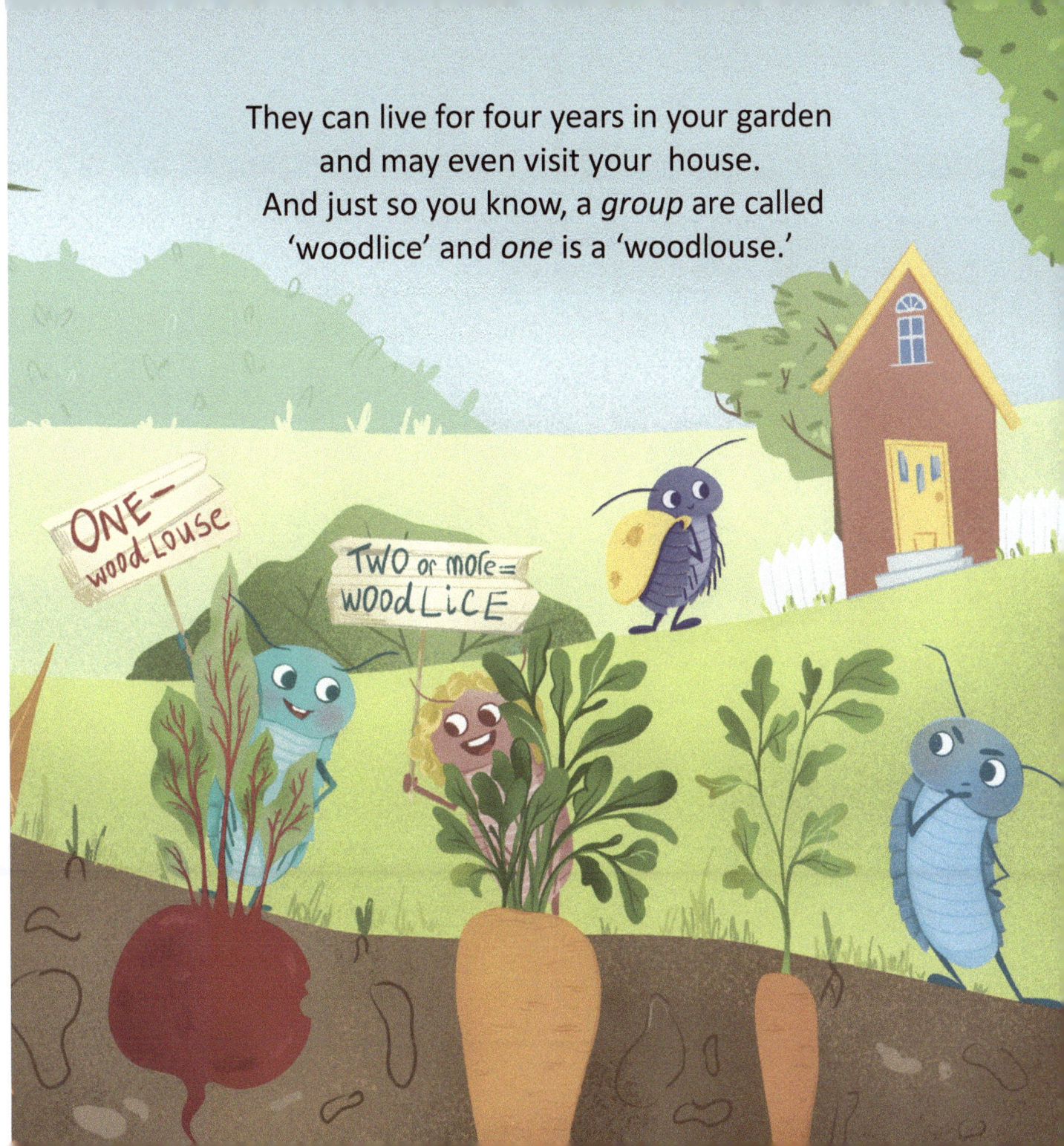

ONE =
wood louse

TWO or more =
wood LICE

When woodlice want to listen to
music, it's not at all odd,
For them to curl up and enjoy
listening to an 'Iso-Pod!'

Oh, see how they dance, those
merry little woodlouse,
As they whirl and twirl to a
waltz by Johann Strauss.

There are over 3500 species of
woodlice that have been found,

OVER 10000 ISOPODS
LIVE HERE

And over 10,000 species of isopod live
in the water and the ground,

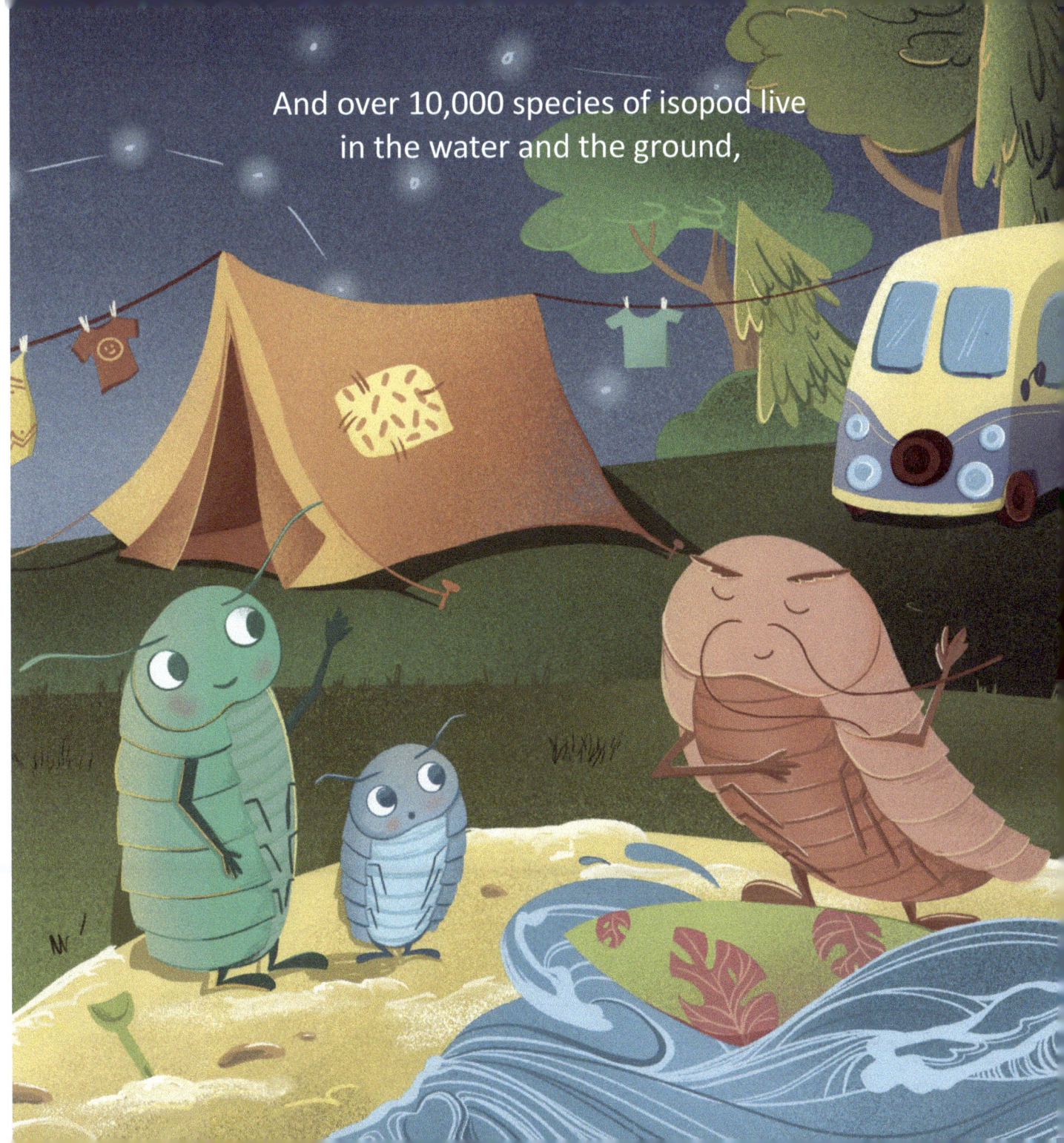

There are real Giant isopods
that live at the bottom of the sea,

They can dwell 7020 feet deep
and grow till they reach 2 foot 3.

7020
↓7020

"Now class, woodlice can give off a rather strong smell. Here are a few in this jar. Sniff, and let's see if you can tell."

NH₃

"They excrete ammonia as gas from their shell.
It's from the waste that they eat to keep them well."

"Miss, I know Isopods use
dead plants as food.
They re-cycle mechanically and
chemically, so everything's renewed."

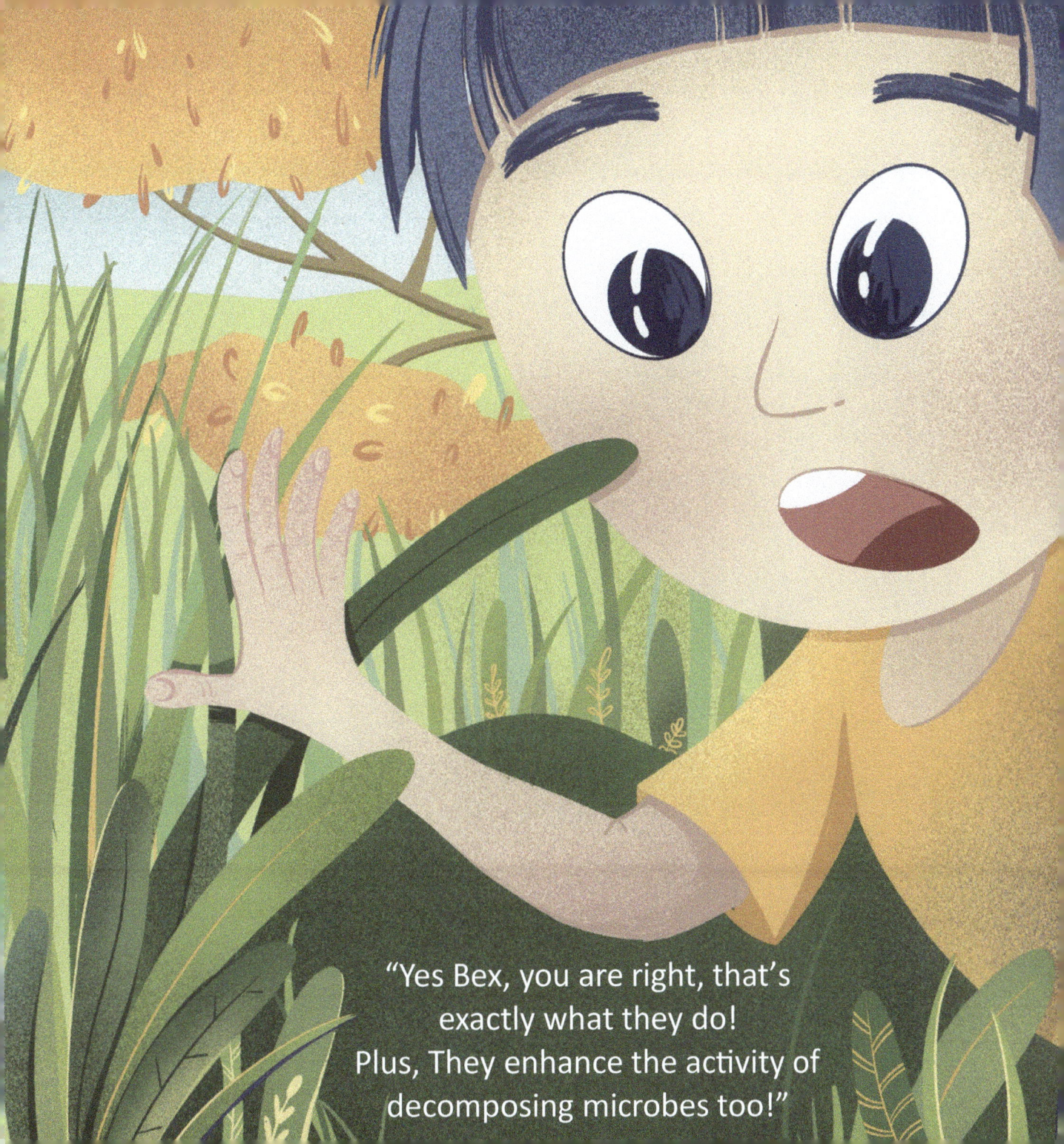

"Yes Bex, you are right, that's
exactly what they do!
Plus, They enhance the activity of
decomposing microbes too!"

OLD TOMATO

Woodlice are nature's tiny gardeners,
also recycling all over you'll see
Like all isopods, they are true friends to
our Earth and to you and to me.

Like chameleons, underwater, isopods can
match their color with where they stay,

This helps them hide from others
who arent as friendly as they say.

DEEP
WATER

Finally, some Isopods are large and
spiny, living very deep indeed.
While others are very small and ride
on fish to help them while they feed.

They have the largest eggs of all
marine invertebrates and as
parents are the 'bees-knees,'
Who come in a range of many
colors that are bound to please.

So now, dear and favourite and inquisitive friend,
this book about woodlice and
other Isopods has come to an end.

From curious crustaceans scuttling
on the seafloor at play,
To the wonderful woodlouse that
you've learnt of today...
We all agree woodlice and all
isopods are happily here to stay!

The End

Woodlice

Woodlouse - plural woodlice - are small isopod crustaceans (creatures without a spine, but have a hard, outer skeleton and a segmented body) that get their name because they are often found in 'old wood.' More fun facts about woodlice are:

1. The common woodlouse, also known as a sowbug, is a species that is surprisingly closely related to crabs and lobsters.
2. Woodlice are harmless. They do not sting or bite or cause any disease
3. They are useful creatures because they only eat decaying matter and, like worms, are one of nature's great recyclers
4. Woodlice are oval and flat and can be brown, grey, or reddish in color
5. Woodlice can live both on water and land. Some species also live in aquatic habitats as they can also breathe underwater using specially adapted gills.
6. Woodlice are herbivores who only survive by eating plants and fruits.
7. According to scientific research, it has been estimated that about 3500 species of woodlouse can be found in the world.
8. The common woodlouse prefers to live in dark and damp places, mainly under the logs or stones. They are also found between walls and in compost heaps.
9. In these dark spaces they often also eat decaying wood.
10. The common woodlouse species can live for three to four years as adults.
11. Do make a good pet
12. One of the best woodlouse facts for children is that a woodlouse is also called a pill bug. This is because when the woodlouse feels threatened, it curls into a ball, showing only its exoskeleton body. This feature where they turn into a ball fascinates everybody!
13. Each species of woodlouse has seven segments in its body, and each segment has one pair of legs. A woodlouse's senses are centered around its eyes and antennae. They have twenty-five individual ocelli in their eyes, which help them to identify large objects

Isopods

Isopods - are crustaceans who can live in the sea, fresh water, or on land. They are cousins of crabs and shrimp. Crustaceans come in many sizes and shapes but what they have in common is that they do not have a spine (invertebrate) and have a hard skeleton on their outside with legs attached to the different segments of their bodies. More fun facts about isopods are:

1. Isopods can be tiny or huge. The giant isopod is one of an estimated 10,000 species of isopods and grows up to 16 inches — making it the largest isopod — while the smallest isopods are just millimeters long
2. Ocean-dwelling isopods have swimming limbs, called pleopods, that they also use for breathing with
3. Isopods are usually gray, brown or black, with an oval-shaped body. They have seven armor plates, called "pereonites," which protect them. They also have seven pairs of short legs. Isopods have two pairs of antennae; one pair feels along the ground.
4. Scientists believe that the average lifespan isopod is around two years. But, there have been examples of these marine creatures living for as long as five years
5. Isopods have various feeding methods: some eat dead or decaying plant and animal matter, others are grazers or filter feeders
6. Some species are able to roll themselves into a ball as a defense mechanism or to conserve moisture.
7. Some isopods, commonly known as rock lice or sea slaters, are the least specialised of the woodlice for life on land. They inhabit the splash zone on rocky shores, jetties and pilings, may hide under debris washed up on the shore and can swim if immersed in water.

David R Morgan lives in England. He is a talented full-time teacher and writer.

He has written music journalism, poetry and children's books. His books for children include : 'The Strange Case of William Whipper-Snapper', three 'Info Rider' books for Collins and 'Blooming Cats' which won the Acorn Award and was animated for television. He has also written a Horrible Histories biography : 'Spilling The Beans On Boudicca' and stories for Children's anthologies.

For the last 5 years he has been working on his Soundings Project with his son Toby, performing his own poetry/writing to Toby's original music. This work is on YouTube, Spotify and Soundcloud.

Other Books by David R. Morgan

Ants are fANTastic
by David R. Morgan

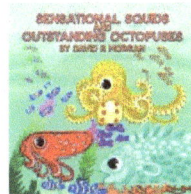
SENSATIONAL SQUIDS AND OUTSTANDING OCTOPUSES
BY DAVID R MORGAN

BUSY BEES AND WILLFUL WASPS
BY DAVID R MORGAN

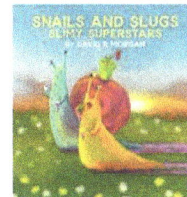
SNAILS AND SLUGS SLIMY SUPERSTARS
BY DAVID R MORGAN

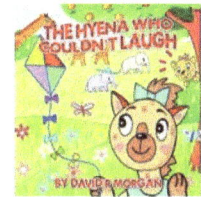
THE HYENA WHO COULDN'T LAUGH
BY DAVID R MORGAN

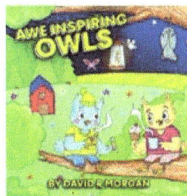
AWE INSPIRING OWLS
BY DAVID R MORGAN

Wonderful Wriggling Whirling Worms
by David R. Morgan

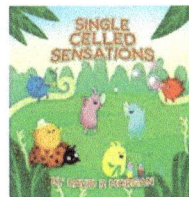
SINGLE CELLED SENSATIONS
BY DAVID R MORGAN

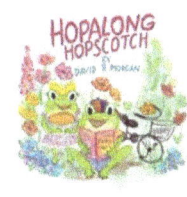
HOPALONG HOPSCOTCH
BY DAVID R MORGAN

Butterfly Beauties and Magical Moths
by David R Morgan

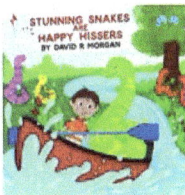
STUNNING SNAKES ARE HAPPY HISSERS
BY DAVID R MORGAN

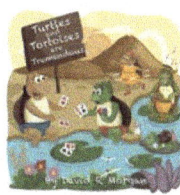
Turtles AND Tortoises ARE Tremendous!
BY DAVID R. MORGAN

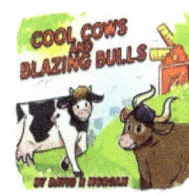
COOL COWS AND BLAZING BULLS
BY DAVID R MORGAN

FABULOUS FROGS AND TERRIFIC TOADS
BY DAVID R MORGAN

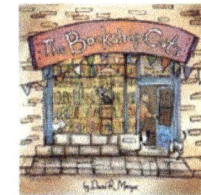
The Barking Cat
by David R Morgan

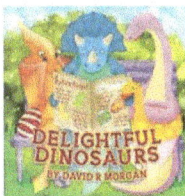
DELIGHTFUL DINOSAURS
BY DAVID R MORGAN

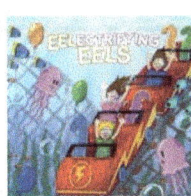
EELECTRIFYING EELS
BY DAVID R MORGAN

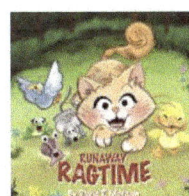
RUNAWAY RAGTIME
By David R Morgan

CRABS ARE inCRABABLE

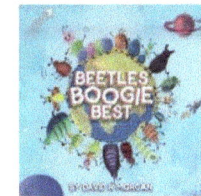
BEETLES BOOGIE BEST
BY DAVID R MORGAN

And many more to come!

More Books by David R. Morgan

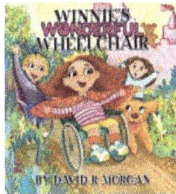

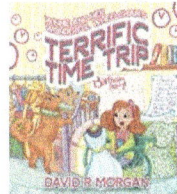

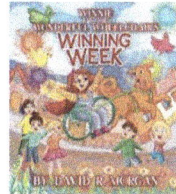

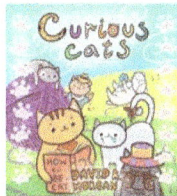

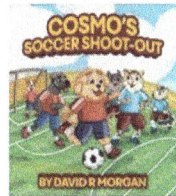

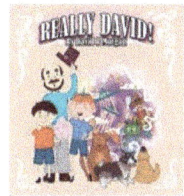

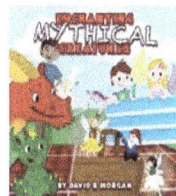

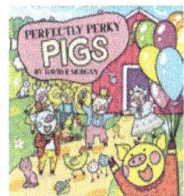

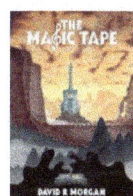

And many more to come!

www.ingramcontent.com/pod-product-compliance
Lightning Source LLC
Chambersburg PA
CBHW042334030426
42335CB00027B/3330